TAKE OUT DELIVERY

PAUL SIEGELL

MW00758237

SPUYTEN DUYVIL
Brooklyn, NY 11211 spuyten
duyvil.net Copyright © 2018 by Paul
Siegell All rights reserved LIBRARY OF
CONGRESS CATALOGING-IN-PUBLICA
TION DATA Names: Siegell, Paul, author. Title:
Take out delivery : po ems and comics / Paul Sie
gell. Description: New York City : Spuyten Duy
vil, [2018] Identifiers: LCCN 2017051561 | IS
BN 9781947980143   (softcover) Classifica
tion: LCC PS3619.   I3838 A6 2018 | D
DC 813/.6—dc23   LC record avail
able at https   ://lccn.loc.
gov/2017   051
561

Cover design by Alexus Encarnado
Lifesaving interior design guidance by Jen Strauss

Lucky Numbers • 9, 11, 9, 11, 9, 1, 11

for Alisa and Linda,
with whom I share
how I am spelled

GINA,

Here's to family!

Paul

«Whooo's got my publisher?» For welcoming these weirdos into The Shared, gratitude:

Apiary Magazine: "WE'VE COME FOR YOUR POETRY READING," "WE'VE COME FOR YOUR TWO-WEEKS NOTICE," "WE'VE COME FOR YOUR WALK-INS WELCOME"

Cleaver Magazine: "WE'VE COME FOR YOUR BLOOD TEST RESULTS," "WE'VE COME FOR YOUR OMMEGANG YAMMERING"

Coconut: "WE'VE COME FOR YOUR COURTESY FLUSH," "WE'VE COME FOR YOUR PROSTATE EXAM," "WE'VE COME FOR YOUR REMOTE CONTROL," "WE'VE COME FOR YOUR SUPPLY & DEMAND"

Cooper Street: "WE'VE COME FOR YOUR SIGNS AND SYMPTOMS"

Dark Sky Magazine: "WE'VE COME FOR YOUR EXTENDED SPINE," "WE'VE COME FOR YOUR SCOUTING REPORT," "WE'VE COME FOR YOUR SPECIAL FORCES"

E·ratio Poetry Journal: "WE'VE COME FOR YOUR MIRRORED MOSAIC"

Everyday Genius: "WE'VE COME FOR YOUR FOOD COURT SAMPLER," "WE'VE COME FOR YOUR HOT AND BOTHERED," "WE'VE COME FOR YOUR MARRIAGE LICENSE," "WE'VE COME FOR YOUR TWO-PERSON TENT"

La Petite Zine: "WE'VE COME FOR YOUR "HEY, HEY, HEY"," "WE'VE COME FOR YOUR LEGEND OF SHIFT+7"

Mad House Magazine: "WE'VE COME FOR YOUR ELITE SQUAD MEMBERS," "WE'VE COME FOR YOUR MELODIOUS THUNK"

No Tell Motel: "WE'VE COME FOR YOUR COPING MECHANISM," "WE'VE COME FOR YOUR GALOSHES," "WE'VE COME FOR YOUR MICROWAVE SAFE," "WE'VE COME FOR YOUR MIRACULOUS MENORAH OIL," "WE'VE COME FOR YOUR WILD TRUTH CASE"

Otoliths: "WE'VE COME FOR YOUR TOP GUN TOWER BUZZ," "WE'VE COME FOR YOUR THERMAL ACTIVITY"

Petite Hound Press: "WE'VE COME FOR YOUR TARGET AUDINCE"

The Portable Boog City Reader: "WE'VE COME FOR YOUR ART EXHIBITION," "WE'VE COME FOR YOUR BURIED TREASURE," "WE'VE COME FOR YOUR PAIN AT THE PUMP," "WE'VE COME FOR YOUR PARTNER IN CRIME," "WE'VE COME FOR YOUR TENT CITY HALL," "WE'VE COME FOR YOUR TRAIN CONDUCTOR HOLE PUNCHER," "WE'VE COME FOR YOUR UNETHICAL TEXTS," "WE'VE COME FOR YOUR UNFATHOMABLE FACT"

Redivider: "WE'VE COME FOR YOUR CARPAL TUNNEL"

Sixth Finch: "WE'VE COME FOR YOUR BOOSTER SHOT," "WE'VE COME FOR YOUR FALLING SKY," "WE'VE COME FOR YOUR SEARCH HISTORY"

Sprung Formal: "WE'VE COME FOR YOUR SUBURBAN URGES"

Sundog Lit: "WE'VE COME FOR YOUR LATE NIGHT LIT," "WE'VE COME FOR YOUR VETERAN AFFAIRS"

Tarpaulin Sky: "WE'VE COME FOR YOUR SURVIVAL SKILLS"

Select comics first appeared in *Antique Children*, *Denver Syntax*, *Moria*, *Otoliths*, and *Word For/Word*. Many thanks to their generous editors.

And, thanks to the graphic and sculptural stylings of Emily Ballas, "WE'VE COME FOR YOUR LEGEND OF SHIFT+7," plus select comics, were featured in **Full Bleed: A Poetry Comics Show**, curated by Hila Ratzabi (Philadelphia, Pa., November 2014).

"Nouns are the name of anything
and just naming names is alright
when you want to call a roll
but is it good for anything else."
　　　　　　—Gertrude Stein

"Their names in your handwriting
are a question of capital letters."
　　　　　　—André Breton

WE'VE COME FOR YOUR UNSPLIT CHOPSTICKS

With runners in scoring position, the fortune cookie I just snapped says, "You can see through people, or see people through." Krist, on the crossword puzzles, queries: "What first starts a heart?" A year from now I am going to tackle realities I never knew, &, hopefully, find myself surviving. To all the sequences encoded within the old, noble sequoia. "Just the facts, ma'am" scavenger hunt. To the comforting scent of a newly sharpened #2 pencil. Passing by in a cork-screw, a cement mixer, aka "HERCULES," honks its horn, hypnotic with "If you can't see my mirrors I can't see you."

WE'VE COME FOR YOUR LATE BREAKING NEWS

"Without action, you aren't going
anywhere."

—*Mahātmā Gandhi*

Calm as a box of bombs, Jay Uxtapo goes: "You can't consume
a can of Campbell's soup, hoping it'll reproduce a reproduction
for you—You gotta believe in it in order to deliver it." Instantly
, the voice of the GPS pops into a nightly news reporter's: "The
phenomenal anonymous." Like a waterwheel ablaze, everything
is of the hunt, voracious. A museum on parade. The sign outside
our culture store reads: "THE NEW TEMPORARY CONTEMP-
ORARY." Photograph. "You and I," the charger purrs to the cell
phone, "we are going into battle. My goal is for you then to win."

WE'VE COME FOR YOUR ACTION FIGURES

"   and go

Talking of Michelangelo."

—T.S. Eliot

Overslept, running down the sidewalk in a comic strip, he's
not the quickest nincompoop in the thingamabob, but knows
it is almost impossible to get through life without stumbling.
A sculpture of turns—Naptime treasure map scavenger hunt.
It all barks back to the Wanted section. There's an emo band
named "LOST DOG" on every other telephone pole in town.
Coming in with a package, she lips to a grin: "Wanna do me
a huge favor? I'm up t'my asses in alligators." As discreet as
cleavage. With a G.I. Joe kung fu grip, he replies: "My *plezh*.
Friends don't let friends fend for themselves." How nice. It's
like I'm one yawn away from "Rip Van Winklin'," but if you
wanna make it in this town: Gotta get to work at 7, leave at 8.

WE'VE COME FOR YOUR COPING MECHANISM

At the tone, please record your message. When you have finished recording you may hang up, or press 1 for more options: *"Having a slight anxiety attack—Call me back!"*

WE'VE COME FOR YOUR EXTENDED SPINE

> "Life isn't just about taking in oxygen
> and giving out carbon dioxide."
> —*Malala Yousafzai*

Inhale: upward facing cat. Exhale to downward dog. It's
healthier to *Namasté* than Tastykake. A woman walks by
with a yoga mat rolled in her bag. Warrior two. Bow and
arrow notebook—Target acquired: shots fired. And from
that minaret, the Minaret of Breath, phthalate-free prayer
rugs unfurl. Sequences tone as if adjustable revelations of
paperclips. Carbo-loaded, my chakras are all full of pasta.
After then it ricochets. Trajectory? Direct to Trader Joe's.

WE'VE COME FOR YOUR LEGEND OF SHIFT+7

"The fullness of life is in the hazards of life."
—*Edith Hamilton*

Zeus pulled his electric chair up to the table saw, clutched
his forklift, his jackknifed tractor trailer, & gorged himself
on a tectonic plate of angel hair & eggplant. Some serving!
Blasé, Ptolemy meh'd the meal, but still the clink of flutes.
What do you mean exactly? scavenger hunt. The Pleiades!
From her penthouse atop the W Hotel, Cassiopeia lovingly
spooned Ptolemy's tapioca from out of Kalamazoo to feed
the ex-Kuala Lumpurians living in Tuscaloosa—When the
ex-Kuala Lumpurians asked for more, she downloaded on-
to them mpegs of the chef show: *Mama Enigma's Cassava*.
& then, after discussing asparagus with Degas after fueling
up for a whirl, Pegasus spun: *How come the comfort of soft
hot pretzels hasn't twisted into ampersands—& vice versa?*

WE'VE COME FOR YOUR CARPAL TUNNEL

> "Name deleted at insistence of
> publisher's lawyer."
> —*Hunter S. Thompson*

It's interesting how there are two ways to write the symbol
for the standard number four: with the triangle and without.
I don't want to give away all of my secrets, but I really like
the look of lowercase f. Similarly, "minimum" is by far one
of my favorites words to cue on a keyboard: down up down
up down up down: Typing! The scavenger hunt, unraveling.
As a set of movements, it can be achingly rhythmic, critical.
"Fashion Week models walking the streets look like aliens."
Somebody typed that—Wasn't me. I just copied & pasted it.

WE'VE COME FOR YOUR "HEY, HEY, HEY"

> "Our lives begin to end the day we become
> silent about things that matter."
> —*Dr. Martin Luther King Jr.*

Huck Finn's adrenalin's kickin' in. Up on the trombone:
Tom Sawyer! And all stellar in their futuristic funkscape
'staches, it's the *Sam Clemens Seven*—Lip-locked to hip
hop—Then, oh baby, Bill Cosby's feelin' it. He snatches
two spoons off the nearest dessert tray: glasses of choco-
late mousse. He licks 'em clean and jiggles down a rapid
series of clicks, jam-slanging iambics on this old paddle-
wheel here, clear across the nightingale... Nonetheless un
-impressed, Fat Albert goes back to howlin' out the blues.

WE'VE COME FOR YOUR POWER PELLETS
—for Elaine

Somewhere, the Pac-Man shirt (my favorite!) that I plopt
into the hamper, but then never saw again once my mama
decided I'd outgrown it, is still size "S" and a-gobblin' up
pixilated poltergeists printed onto cotton. "There's no rea-
son to put away the wonder," Jimi Hendrix says to his sky
-eyed *Tyrannosaurus rex*. Pterodactyl scavenger hunt. Re:
"Do you recall the first time you were introduced to silver
dollar pancakes?" Betsy Ross asks Baryshnikov. "There's
a chomp monster in everyone," he declares. "My *favorite*!"

pork chop
sit-ups?

tae kwon do
takedowns!

hot pepper people
tearing open must-read
mustard packets

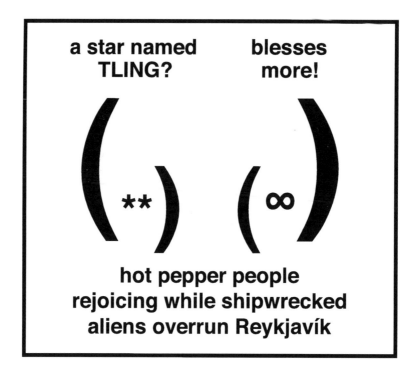

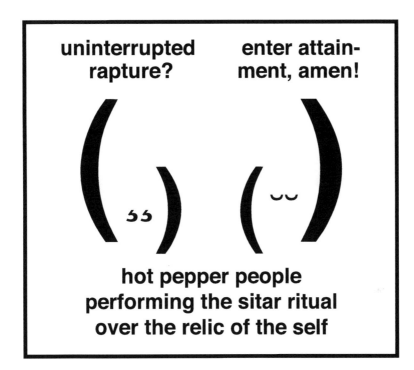

WE'VE COME FOR YOUR INTRO TO INTERPERSONAL COMMUNICATIONS

> "I like physics, but I love cartoons."
> —*Stephen Hawking*

Hi. Sharp as a DIXON *TICONDEROGA* on test day: that awkward moment when you first shake hands with someone, then immediate -ly space their name. Heh? Sharing the shenanigans, they've got no clue what yours is either, so that's exciting. "—Pleased to meet you , whoever you are." Gentlemen Jack scavenger hunt. The politeness of spies. Some sounds are more valuable than others. Even *Steven*'s.

WE'VE COME FOR YOUR ELITE SQUAD MEMBERS

—for Luke Kasdan-Codd

"Balls!" Rachmaninoff cries. "I haven't written a roam in weeks!" TomTom, petty. Tom Petty a-tumbleweeds to a friend in need. Be —The rocker rolls up, yee-haws a "Hop on!" and away they prey: He'd just puff'd some poltergeist grass. In the backseat, Kokopelli puts down his pipe and whispers, "*I, I can do in-cred-i-ble things.*" Avenue of the Arts scavenger hunt. "*And we, we all know you can, too.*" Wings out: *Flight Forth*. The radio speaks: "If these findings hold up, then it is perfectly reasonable that each should be encouraged to masturbate." Kokopelli sips his pipe—Then with a gesture exactly the opposite to a quiver's equivalent, the pianist succumbs , "Man, today's been like one wild pitch after another... *Yee-haw!*"

WE'VE COME FOR YOUR SCOUTING REPORT

> "I can't picture people talking about
> me 50 years from now."
>
> —*Sandy Koufax*

Up, Gorbachev recently revealed that he was a huge fan of Tug McGraw, said he was akin to "A bioluminescent leviathan—A stallion on the mound." What are the odds on another October? I find myself gazing upon a stained glass window—A carousel of traffic lights for ballerinas with varicose veins. My feet are sweating and blathering on about leaping us skyward, off the diamond. A mosaic of stadiums rocked to the tune of *Sputnik 1* broadcasting a song of old Rasputin. Final score: Baseball's beautiful.

WE'VE COME FOR YOUR ART EXHIBITION

"Exaggerate the essential, leave
the obvious vague."

—*Vincent Van Gogh*

On a day when I shaved myself into uneven sideburns,
ladies and gentlemen, my latest obsession: the tornado-
pagoda of her ribcage to the fierce soft sculpture of her
hair. "Visions of Johanna" scavenger hunt. "You know
I'm at my absolute best," says the frenemy of her schiz-
ophrenia, "when dancing—A red-ruckus love shack of
lobsters during an earthquake; 'at's my next move, so."

WE'VE COME FOR YOUR FOOD COURT SAMPLER

—for Rob Rynkewicz

General Tso charged himself into Kentucky Fried Chicken's
Louisville headquarters & demanded to speak to the Colonel.
Coleslaw cuts. Threats to bomb rice farmers were made. Was
advised that all the awful organisms of Food Safety warnings
would be unleashed upon KFC if their staffers didn't cease ill-
egally dumping their leftover lo mein takeout cartons into the
fragile habitat of the "EAT MOR CHIKIN" cows—Seriously
? Gag order scavenger hunt. "When the stork stops delivering
all that New York deli," cried the Col., "then we'll talk about
how admirable each of us will be—At any rate, did you bring
any of that low sodium soy sauce with you? We just ran out."

WE'VE COME FOR YOUR FALLING SKY

—for Glenn Gordon Wood

"IMPORTANT! FedEx Express pickup and delivery service in Haiti is suspended until further notice." Via email: "Take a breath," my old summer camp reminded, "and know why."

WE'VE COME FOR YOUR TARGET AUDIENCE

> "No people come into possession of a culture
> without having paid a heavy price for it."
> —*James Baldwin*

That these, these aren't even the things I care about the most.
It's 1 a.m. and I am deleting the death of a poet. Sky burial 5.
What else would I be doing if I just didn't show up for work?
I can see Orion taking aim. St. Sebastian scavenger hunt. On
a walk around the monument today, caged in scaffolding, all
its points of departure: Eve balancing an apple upon her head
while William Tell quarrels Cupid: It is a study in Rayonism.
It is a study in the sting our cash registers supply by opening.

WE'VE COME FOR YOUR MICROWAVE SAFE

"[T]he hope of a skinny kid with a funny name who believes that America has a place for him, too."

—*Barack Hussein Obama II*

In one free-fall after another, Geronimo plants bombs on the U.S. in 3D. Fatherlands cut punk tracks to calm crocodiles at night in their cradles. Crib notes—Sketchpad scavenger hunt. William Carlos Williams knows all the right words and those bold specimens of natural selection say, "Penetrate the glaze." Outside a rowdy happy hour at the Karl Marx Confectionary Factory, a jogger's untangling her headphone wires. They tip nothing about being asleep to the possibilities of insomnia in the recession, but nevertheless invite my minefields to sprout sundials at every new nuking of butter-flavored popcorn bags.

WE'VE COME FOR YOUR SPECIAL FORCES

> "What is important is to spread
> confusion, not eliminate it."
> —*Salvador Dalí*

I'm not sure about the juxtaposition of that Gestapo officer
& the Buddha's Bo tree. Ripping off all the buffalo's limbs
except its wings. Even if World War II knows W.H. Auden
oughtn't be toyed with, B.A. Baracas still pities all the car-
casses he finds—Stark raving mad scavenger hunt—People
of the latest aftermath: a crowd of kids gathers on the street
while their parents wonder what to feed them all for dinner.

WE'VE COME FOR YOUR VETERANS AFFAIRS

"We live in the midst of alarms."
—*Abraham Lincoln*

Mocked by the Washington monument, the hippopotamus in
the Potomac River has DuPont Circle all up in a headlock. A
flag with one red stripe sliced off. The question mark of body
parts—Backstabbing, a scavenger hunt. Female bathers frolic
in the pre-World War III era to the pitter-patter of the caption
: "Tiny coffins among hundreds at quake funeral." After suck-
ing his nails to taste the dirt from underneath, a homeless man
tics, "It doesn't it don't most matter if I know the news or not."

WE'VE COME FOR YOUR PROSTATE EXAM

—for Kristy Pucci

Why not? It's not like any of us are doing anything anyway.
A yellow lab named "Boomer" steps outta his yellow snow.
Bald spots shimmer in the lights at the concert. By the time
she reached the age, she said, that songs were something to
be desired, the only vinyl record in her mother's collection
that wasn't opened: still in cellophane: was Crosby, Stills &
Nash. "The promoted," the box office nods, "is reality now.
Deadline is upon us." Happy Birthday scavenger hunt. All I
can think of is Young, but of all the kidding about the down-
pour of pressure that's produced when, *, a finger gets stuck
inside the situation—Up we woke and went to the bathroom.

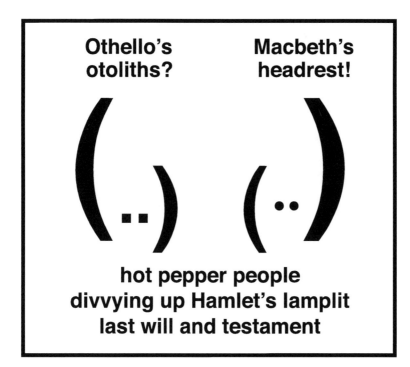

chaos
cicada?

impulse
octopus!

(ħħ) (өө)

hot pepper people
tightening up
their grooviest of shoelaces

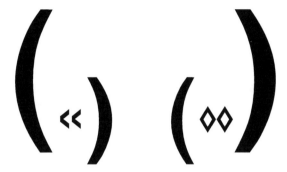

scantily clad free radicals? post-apocalyptic pickpockets! hot pepper people running riot at a massive, six-turntable spectacular

WE'VE COME FOR YOUR THERMAL ACTIVITY

> "I really miss being able to blend in with people."
> —*Kurt Cobain*

They just put it up. The large banner hanging outside the world famous Ming Dynasty Museum and Mineral Hot Springs reads: "*Wyoming Welcomes Ernest Hemingway!*" It's all gonna go over like a fart in church. Somebody just called, asked, "Is the undertaker there?" Deadbeat dad scavenger hunt. His daughter replied, "*Well, fire up a pack of adjectives!*" As passionate about Picasso as M.C. Escher was about deciphering the square root of a sculpture garden, Jay Uxtapo strip'd down to his leopard print Speedo and said, "Said properly, our names: the hallowing of time: who."

WE'VE COME FOR YOUR WILD TRUTH CHASE
"That which was hidden worried them."
—*Jackson Mac Low*

Mao Tse-tung walked into Walmart looking for bullet ideas.
He overheard a mother lol, "But the piss can't go in the gar-
bage disposal," and immediately exited the automatic doors:
Too much confusion in the cockpit—With a wheelbarrow of
mini marshmallows, Mickey Mantle couldn't find the things
he thought weren't lost—Flights of "Which?" Such a shame.
He'd hoped it was all gonna go away—Like a lot of life, no?
Helicopters evacuate war-wounded soldiers in his heartbeats.
To look out for later. Look for something that looks like this:
Travesty scavenger hunt—"What aisle the new Mattel toys?"

WE'VE COME FOR YOUR "SPOOKTACULAR"

"The first fiction is your name."
—*Eileen Myles*

It's all a Halloween show: Everyone's in costume—The
Trojan horse knows what I'm talking about. Heightening
the absurdity, "Let's score some road kill," rip'd Charles
Barkley, "and bring it to the party!" Naturally, he offered
that while sporting Bob Marley dreads. I & I, like the *"I"*
inside the "We," the trick-or-treaters keep ghouling back
to our house because there are a lotta happy horrors here.
Vlad says, "You look about as ridiculous as my mother."
"Are you," asks a Doublemint, "my people-person twin?"
Jack-o'-lantern scavenger hunt—Name-dropping TV sets.
Would be no "HOLLYWOOD" without 'em. Reanimate!

WE'VE COME FOR YOUR TOP GUN TOWER BUZZ

—for MediaLab

"Now, stars, underneath this Hello Kitty Band-Aid, adorable red bow in tow, is the ever-tender flesh wound that Emily Dickinson 's writing hand snagged while horsing around with Joan of Arc." Readjust. Banned books scavenger hunt. By the flick you figure out onto which shelf they go, your co-pilot has long since hit the fasten seat belt sign—To moisten the voices, lest we want Eddie Vedder to ring out the Riot Act, now is a good time to set the artificial insemination of all the existential oyster shells into action: As if Bruce Lee hi-ho-silvering Rudolf the Red-Nosed Reindeer, been a gigantic fly swooping a ruckus over my Mac all morning.

WE'VE COME FOR YOUR TELEPORT PASSPORT

> "I wish I could write a beautiful book to break
> those hearts that are soon to cease to exist."
> —*Zelda Fitzgerald*

By the time Botticelli learned how to ollie on his skateboard, Caravaggio had already performed his fourth cello recital. O, those precocious getters of the go—It's homies like those that Vermeer reveres the most. In an effort to appease the druthers of the suburbs, "Volvos!" he cries. "We need more Volvos up in this piece—Safety first, you know?" Ahh, Europa. It's like: "*Toilet seats?* Where *we're* going, we don't *need* toilet seats." Without a paddle scavenger hunt. But with Venus now in retro -grade, FedEx Tracking says the copy of *Medusa, The Gorgon of Google (Vol. VI)* that I overnighted should be arriving at 27 rue de Fleurus any minute now. The expats have been waiting.

WE'VE COME FOR YOUR PARTNER IN CRIME

> "It's better to be unhappy alone
> than unhappy with someone."
> —*Marilyn Monroe*

& like a proctologist for a pterodactyl, this one's gonna involve *shrieking*—Instead of doing it to his new BMW, Courtney Love keyed the side of Odysseus' kayak. She hoped it'd do more dam -age. Jack the Ripper scavenger hunt. Shot sloppiness. Of all the things that a diamond demands, but how *does* one involve more LOVE? The eyes of enchantment are like two mazes encased in a sunset lake. A hint of firmament, a foreshadow to a silhouette: It's OK to make a promise, then be timid that you did. For when Odysseus enticed the Sirens, they sang for him George Harrison, harmonizing to each soothing hallelujah, each modest adoration. But when Courtney arrived, they plugged her in to Bruce Spring -steen, then struck the chord—*"Everybody's gotta hungry heart."*

WE'VE COME FOR YOUR HOT AND BOTHERED
—for Pooch, again

The firemen are *feelin' effin' irie, mon*. Out hums one a-the
younger ones: moseys up to the ice cream truck, orders two
Strawberry Shortcakes, three Choco Tacos & a Rocket pop.
Rook to Queen's Knight Five—Black King scavenger hunt.
Set to summon the Jedi mind trick, Darth Vader holds forth
his grim, gloved hand, but this time R2PeePoo & StinkTPO
were impenetrable. They had found the secret. "Not today,"
bleep-blopped the little one. All Vader wanted was for them
to grab him a Chipwich—Gets so hot for him inside his suit.

WE'VE COME FOR YOUR REMOTE CONTROL

"Say my name."
—*Beyoncé*

Blazing chimera chimichangas!—Taking New Orleans to new extremes: on a Super Bowl of old en *Español*—Playing catch-up tackling blue corn tortilla chips, Roger Waters' mouth goes dry: *Tequila?*—*Si!* Click to a small college crowd cheering up an epic ping-pong battle. Action-packed scavenger hunt. Wild rivals sweating in the unpredictable. Who'll win? In my expert opinion: "*Yo no sé, no sé*—" yet the drop of rain that's dancing the salsa as a splash upon a mountaintop does, however, know from the oceans: reckon Frosty the Snowman, or Henry David Thoreau. Fresh-caught fish tacos. And as fluid as another news show covering the Gulf of Mexico, but showing where another nor'easter is set to strike, before a bored Waters flips it back to the game, the subtitle tips: "to how hurricanes get their names."

WE'VE COME FOR YOUR BIRTH OF WORDPLAY
—for Roy & J.P. Rosenbaum

When I was cut from hers, I made a sound and was given to him and they made me a sound—They gave me growth and made sounds so I could sound more like them. Many others came with every shining, and I made sounds with others old and new to sound—Leaks happened when sounds happened when it was hard to see. When others uttered the purpose of sound that I was made, I made the yes of sound. Strange and then OK when someone else said yes to the sound that I was made because I listened enough to know that that sound was mine, but also his and shared. Every shining gave me growth and one shining I was with another who was made the sound that I identified, but instead of it being the first of his sounds, *it lived between his others*; for he also honored a third: a last: a brand: & he shared that fact with a bigger other who shared such care with him, who being bigger called me "P.a.u.smell."

WE'VE COME FOR YOUR SURVIVAL SKILLS

> "What is disagreeable and offends my modesty
> is that at bottom I am every name in history."
> —*Friedrich Nietzsche*

What happens when through a wormhole a gravestone passes?
Does it matter how fit the biography? Arc, longevity in a time
warp? How many other people know your name, or image, or
oeuvre? "For the love of G-d!" cries Ancient Mesopotamia. "
Would you put your *John Hancock* on that Word .doc already
?" Peace Pact scavenger hunt—For good or ill [and to a fault]:
this Jell-O brick road, this far-fetched fête of world-renowned
proper nouns: our masquerade: this Internet connection to that
which could easily be found in any given graphic art scenario:
Then why not poetry, too? "'What's for breakfast?' said Pooh."

WE'VE COME FOR YOUR UNETHICAL TEXTS

"Is your name by any chance Rumpelstiltskin?"
—*Anne Sexton*

Might on the rise. Like stirring sheets of Kierkegaard into
a tank of kerosene, everything is primed for a sonic boom.
Sounds like a job for F. Scott Prescott, Esquire—He asks,
"What keeps you going?" Al Capone jokes, "Up up down
down left right left right B A start?" Now, Napoleon's pet
emperor penguin is duking it out with Punxsutawney Phil.
Flabbergast scavenger hunt—Not a real huge fan of spring
that one, but either way, when they come out of the printer,
the poems hug the heat like towels from a dryer just abuzz.

WE'VE COME FOR YOUR INDEPENDENT BOOKSTORE

> "O who will pump these breasts?
> I cannot waltz my tongue."
> —*Sonia Sanchez*

CAConrad comes into the bar and unloads how he just swallowed a brick of C4 explosives. Frank Sherlock starts singing, "Drinking gin with Kerouac. Drinking Jack with Ginsberg—And stop giving us telephone books, nutbags!" *Anna Karenina* scavenger hunt. It's nights like this that (*Yo, what's up?*) the strobe light swerves to flit and the spike overflows the satyrs all over, and anyone with a book published by a small press unzips their nipples: then set to sting the Oprah of our senses, out come the alchemical penmanship jellyfish.

WE'VE COME FOR YOUR TENT CITY HALL

> "I don't create chaos. I merely
> deal with it."
>
> —*Johnny Rotten*

"Mic check / MIC CHECK!" Sign says, "I *have* a college degree. I *am* employed. I *have* showered—I *am* still here! Next stereotype?" Sign says, "Stay focused—Don't let us become another Tea Party." Sign says, "The truth will not be televised!" Sign says, "TOP 1%, Y U NO *PAY TAXES?*" Capture the flag scavenger hunt—Crowd chants, "*We are! the 99%—And so are you!*" Crowd chants, "*Police! Come join us—They want your pensions, too!*" The People chant as unemployed neighbors fear front lawn foreclosure signs , as Wall St unapologetically sprays democracy in the face, as corporate jets fuel up on bonuses: #OccupyEverywhere!

WE'VE COME FOR YOUR KILLER KICK DRUM
—for Ernest Hilbert

CBGB & OMFUG bottom their bottles to the sound of an
engine running: Joey & Johnny rarin' to go. Torn, Sheena
screams, "*Ezra, my head is throbbing!*" But we got tickets
because MUSIC is the prescription drug of music therapy.
Rat-a-tat-tat scavenger hunt. W/Burroughs nearby, Debbie
Harry's bra strap flirts a fall. Patti Smith slides in for a fix.
In purple permanent marker she writes, "*What will we end
up wearing?*" onto her thigh. Indie. Incendiary. "Uplifting
Gormandizers" underground: Voltage crackles at the edge.

WE'VE COME FOR YOUR BOOSTER SHOT

> "I wish so much to go that I almost wish
> I had never been there."
>
> —*Georgia O'Keeffe*

It's almost naptime at Neptune's, but the painters are waiting
to ship off their pigments and visions—Shamans unsure who
they should tap to handle such a ridiculously critical delivery
: NASA or NASCAR? Taxicab scavenger hunt—From all the
bohemian haunts of Montmartre to all the gardens of curiosity
within Golden Gate Park, I realize not everyone gets the same
thing outta the same sentence, but what's the point of wasting
gas by racing to a red light? O, the Hologram of Here and the
Telegram of There: This was sent to me, but was really meant
for you: A beige being I'll be no more—*Ah, put rockets on it!*

WE'VE COME FOR YOUR LIQUID DIAL SOAP

> "I had also done a little disc jockeying."
> —*Casey Kasem*

Volume me, Emanuel: "And that bust-out was the Talking Heads with their influential 'Radio Head.' Comin' at you next is Queen with 'Radio Ga Ga.'" Fab Four scavenger hunt. She hit "SCAN" and then landed on a frequency halfway through "Lady Sings the Blues." Louise goes, *Whoa! Hold up a sec... It was either Grandma Sue, or Johnny Cash, but someone wasn't wearing skin in my dream last night*—From her moves, an avalanche of lavender—I didn't know what to do with all that, so I just changed the station.

WE'VE COME FOR YOUR BLOOD TEST RESULTS

"I wish to go on living even after my death."

—*Anne Frank*

On the bridge, the birdgirl waits with a weight in her ribcage.
Symbolically, a sailor and his sweetheart. A sparrow pecking
at a cigarette. A sparrow pecking at salt for snow. Next to the
pizza place, she keys up a door with a horseshoe over it, then
goes to sleep with hair clips in—Like the firepower rainwater
has on Fort Torch Falls, the level rises in a surge—Exhausted
, she whispers into her pillow: "*Bring me wings to beat, burn.*"

WE'VE COME FOR YOUR POETRY READING

> "And that's our job. It's to spark
> somebody else watching us."
> —*Tupac Shakur*

Of all the numerous rumors within Philadelphia's bricks,
a sticker on our STOP sign says, "I shapeshift to a spliff."
What I do not know reaches immeasurability, but what I
am aware of is that sometimes I'm not invited to the new
because I never attended the old—It can be discouraging
, to be ignored. Deep impact scavenger hunt. But to leave
yrself out, that's just irresponsibility. Wait: of all the bull-
dogs being blogged about, I heard someone go: "Kiss her
psyche; do so every day." Prescription? Pendulum clocks.

WE'VE COME FOR YOUR MIRRORED MOSAIC

> "It still may take some explaining, but many
> more women are keeping their birth names."
> —*Gloria Steinem*

Wedding a palace of glass to the princess cut of a diamond in
the rough: a bathtub of light bulbs—When he felt no one was
watching, the Candy Man amok'd about the sparkle carnival
under Matisse's mattress. All through the tunnels and grottos,
he crafted sweet reminders of a life engaged with inspiration,
while Isaiah Zagar wondered, "What happens when you look
inside?" South Street's Magic Garden scavenger hunt. Elated,
like something astounding's happening: We direct electricity.
Off a wall, Isaiah expressed, "Your light excels by shattering.
I collide. I can't imagine a more exquisite wedding for a ring."

WE'VE COME FOR YOUR OMMEGANG YAMMERING

"The world was to me a secret
which I desired to divine."
—*Mary Shelley*

Frank O'Hara has a few nosey people coming over: "It's a party!"
he announces, then into the parking garage he disappears like the
Boston Bruins blowing a three-games-to-none lead in the Stanley
Cup playoffs to the Philadelphia Flyers. To my knowledge, Frank
Zappa isn't being played in any of the elevators in O'Hara's build-
ing, but, *yeah*, most likely still lingering up there are my 11th floor
farts—Child caregivers beware: goes a man painting famous faces
onto a hotdog cart, tryna get them to blend into the murals of Dirty
Frank's Bar. And of his Franz Kafka kasha recipe? An approxima-
tion. It's missing something: Aretha on the juke? Ben on the stove
? Rabble-rouser scavenger hunt. Flying kites, we still don't know,
so we're left to wonder right when we need to least—The last line
of my horoscope reads, "Walk away without any words, for now."

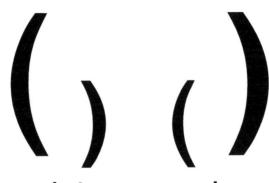

**hot pepper people
silenced by the tastiness
of stone crab claws**

hubbub in the bathtub?   **breathe thru your bowels!**

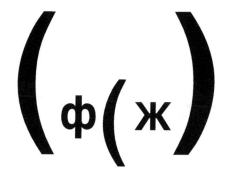

**hot pepper people
tryna stay away from the
meningitis in the margins**

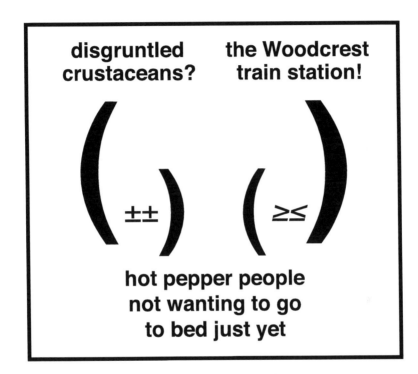

WE'VE COME FOR YOUR TRAIN CONDUCTOR HOLE PUNCHER

—for Nick Pugliese

Psychotic eye sockets: everyone Amtrak-aiming elsewhere.
From above, the rush hour train station looks like a Jackson
Pollock: paint drips of people being whipped about by time.
Traveling salesmen scavenger hunt—But what's even odder
is... 111,111,111 x 111,111,111 = 12,345,678,987,654,321. I
don't even try to figure out how it works; I just say, "Wow!"

WE'VE COME FOR YOUR COURTESY FLUSH
—for Darreth & Mike Zeccardi

—And it goes like this: Dude on his cell phone: "I don't give a shit!" Laxative scavenger hunt. "O.K! Effin' a—Whatever. I'll see you later." On a protester's sign, "I AM NOT YOUR ATM" reminds me that some people just simply desire desire. I edited a PowerPoint presentation on it once. Idea being that there's always at least one asshole around, anywhere you go. Was kind of a "*Muchas gracias, Captain Obvious!*" moment , but so true at the same time. All the same, I'll take time out to time take out vs. dine in, but never dine in a place that puts the toilet paper on the toilet paper holder all wrong. Flushing, Dairy Queen plays quid pro quo with Don Quixote: "Around and around we go! Here's to all our *Hungry Hungry Hippos!*"

WE'VE COME FOR YOUR SIGNS AND SYMPTOMS

> "An artist is somebody who produces things
> that people don't need to have."
>
> —*Andy Warhol*

Leashed to two black labs, he kicks with two white cords fixed
to his ears. A deviant da Vinci device. "Add to cart." Feels like
I throw everything away; even my garbage cans are plastic—In
anticipation… of yet another ransacking of RadioShack, Quasi-
modo provokes Yoko Ono: "You do, don't you?" Yes, I'm only
just aiming at making a Self for my name, but my tongue is like
a patient afraid of slipping on Freud. *Jabberjaw* scavenger hunt.
Thanks, mom! Outside of the hospital, the doctor lays her stetho
-scope around her neck just as the battery beats it on my iPhone.

WE'VE COME FOR YOUR WALK-INS WELCOME

> "Sometimes one pays most for the things
> one gets for nothing."
>
> —*Albert Einstein*

As I flip in and out of lost and found, my human search for the balance of a mind at peace ponders what the level of existence is within its self. So to jettison the emptiness, up I ambulanced across the bridge to speak with the lighthouse keeper: SORRY WE'RE CLOSED. For Rent. NO PARKING. It's one of those "*Only the lotus knows*," y'know? Abracadabra scavenger hunt. A mind-boggling blogger. Nonsense and a long time since, the idiot within strikes again! Ah, well: after red I lift my leg, shift it to the right, so my body will resume moving forward: *faster!*

WE'VE COME FOR YOUR GALOSHES

—for the Perki Turkies

The law firm of "Leary, Kesey & Wolfe" has more liquid assets
than Niagara Falls. *Also Sprach Zarathustra*—"Did anyone else
just spot that Sasquatch?" I reveled—Answer: "Me and Harpua."
Going bowling with a roll of toilet paper, there's a No smOKing
sign on my book of matches. Last year at the Folk Festival, Luke
revealed, "A funny thing to say to someone on acid:" He pointed
to the ground and then, *"Get outta the fire ants!"* Outside's a guy
who just inadvertently spit on his dick while seducing the urinal,
waiting for piss. A sneeze and he liberates the outcome of his last
draught submitted for approval. Chem lab scavenger hunt. Gutter
ball, but then a spare—Wondering what's to pick inside my nose,
it smells like someone had asparagus then peed all over the place.

WE'VE COME FOR YOUR SUBURBAN URGES

"Tastes so good, cats ask for it by name."
—*Meow Mix*

Pondering the difference between adolescents in Albu-
querque playing classic *Super Mario Bros.* in slippery
vintage nylon Umbro shorts, or a scenario of adults go
-in' balls-out *bukkake* at the back of the all-*nuevo* New
Mexicano Kabuki Theatre, Catherine the Great queues
up another sweet reason to masturbate. Of the whirr &
succulence. Scantily clad scavenger hunt. But... that'll
have to linger: First, she's gotta run to the dry cleaners
& then the bank—& then pick the kids up from school.

WE'VE COME FOR YOUR TWO-PERSON TENT
—for Marc Kantrowitz & Josh Beale

A few weeks ago, Leonardo DiCaprio dreamed that Cleopatra was hosting a karaoke night at the KOA Kampsite just outside Des Moines, Iowa—Lust was inevitable. So was the "OUT OF ORDER" sign that Renoir painted on the outhouse door. They were giving pretzels for prizes, but instead of salt they had hot pepper flakes from the Chiropractor factory, which helped him make sense of why, wild in the next site over, Pontius, that old crux, was doing Pilates. Chili's baby back ribs scavenger hunt. Weird thing was: he had the exact same dream again last night.

WE'VE COME FOR YOUR BUSINESS CASUAL

—for Ariel Rosemberg

To a dude in a "DECOLONIZE EDUCATION" tee, a woman in a pink hijab asks, "How much of this was here before it was discovered?" Their lack of an apathetic attitude makes me look bad. Today's been the busiest day I've had in months—Am I allowed to say "Cluster fuck" on air, or will that just toss the boss off into too much chaos? *¡Y mucho más!* Clicks, it's currently a sunny 76 in Jackson Hole, Wyo. *¡Espectacular!* scavenger hunt. In an I.M. my friend in Atlanta *blechs*: "The thought of Justin Bieber in my town is whatever the opposite of mINdblowINg is!" Me: "That's what's crappenin'!" Coming up next hour on the program, I've a few more live Dead tracks of "St. Stephen" to staple together. My coworker goes, "It sure makes the day go faster, though; don't it?"

WE'VE COME FOR YOUR TWO-WEEKS NOTICE

"So Romeo would, were he not Romeo call'd,
Retain that dear perfection."

—*William Shakespeare*

"Git!" a tour guide recently signaled: "You gotta take your foot off first to steal second." A breath, pitch—That oomph and its "Go-Go-Gadget Yo!" reinforced the handful of path-advancing risks I've taken in the past few years; & likewise, how those major gambles brought me here: the finest office environment from which I have benefitted to date. Thing is, I believe in the ol' "Gain. Maintain. And Then Gain Again." It's time. It comes with candid sadness, yet wild enthusiasm, that I present this letter of intention to tender my resignation: On the right track scavenger hunt. Thus, I throw myself back at the whims of the HR Director of the Ancients, and keep in mind when Emerson ev'ryoned: "The things that are for thee gravitate to thee." Respectfully Yours, And the runner goes >

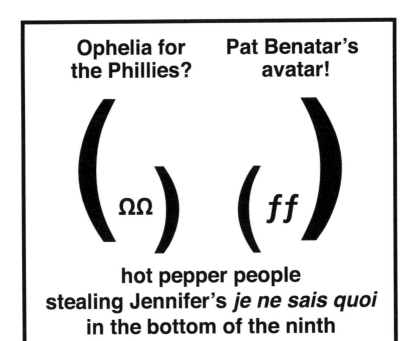

why can't i keep my eyes open?

the Dutch Oven will see you now!

(zz)   (≠≠)

hot pepper people
flipping it to the cold
side of the pillow

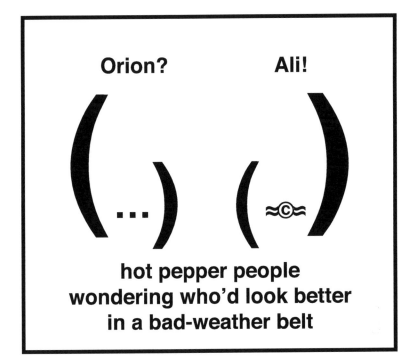

WE'VE COME FOR YOUR PAUSE BUTTON

"Fire and smoke engulf the towers of the World," a caption
begins—One of the saddest scavenger hunts ever imagined.
Things we don't think about while listening to Pink Floyd's
"Us and Them." Another JFK-like day. "Others leaped from
the windows as the structures fell," from another color photo
-graph. In no sense, they came for our innocent: "United We
Stand." I take off my belt and shoes going through the x-ray
scanner. I put on my patriotism going through my fears, then
my cynicism going through the motions. I'd read about a put
-on while going into war, but will forever pay my respects at
the sites of the fallen, all of those names engraved to tragedy.

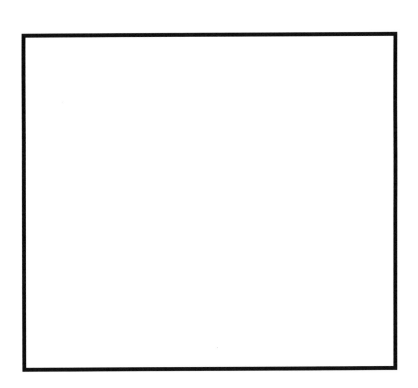

WE'VE COME FOR YOUR UNFATHOMABLE FACT

"I recognized my name when I saw it."
—*Joan Didion*

When Man Ray heard how a stingray spine pierced the chest
of the *Crocodile Hunter*, he stumbled back in his studio, took
off his Ray-Ban mirrors, turned down the Sun Ra record, and
collapsed. Their friendship, pearlescent; its shimmer fed them
full—Manna from Heaven scavenger hunt—When he came to
, the artist to a blank canvas raced and, as if an ominous grand
piano silencing a star, he ferociously blackened everything out.

WE'VE COME FOR YOUR PAIN AT THE PUMP

> "I am just one human being."
> —*The Dalai Lama*

The Maya counted on it, so we rode the merry-go-round till
we reached the Skeleton Stop. Back lit: the skull of a horse.
"It's largely a mystery, but you must youth yourself against
your ghost." Balancing act scavenger hunt. Some centering:
The highway outta Manhattan makes me want to make sure
I've got my charger on me; it makes me want to reconsider
: "Most of those being found," announces CNN, "are dead."

WE'VE COME FOR YOUR MARRIAGE LICENSE

> "The real names of our people were
> destroyed during slavery."
> —*Malcolm X*

With her machine gun soaking in breast milk, Zoe is smoking
Marlboros before the Ouroboros. I put my prayers in zero—A
laughingstock on TV, H.D. took an arrow to the elbow, hasn't
been the same since—Johnnie Cochran holds up the cock ring
, shows the jury, calls it "Exhibit X." Tattletale scavenger hunt.
"That's diabolical," he says. "Well, sayonara, Aram Saroyan!"
Is it time yet to drive the Bronco out onto the freeway? O.J. in
the locker room goes, "No worries. I won't leave without you."

WE'VE COME FOR YOUR HIGH WIRE ACT

> "I wanted to make carnival rides. That
> was my big ambition."
>
> —*Red Grooms*

Bluffing a flush until the Queen of Hearts painted the river,
a Mad Hatter who can't stop shaking his legs. I don't even
think he's aware of it—Hidden agendas all across America
. Insanity plea scavenger hunt—I got the "Overblown Cele
-brity Wedding Blues," but it's just another day at the cere-
monies for the mad-red grooms and the wandering eyes of
their mail-order brides: *And that's Las Vegas for ya!* Little
white chapel fiascos of Elvis, ATM fees and a grand buffet
of questionable decisions. And you? What are your where-
abouts about? Feels like it's time to get going on letting go.

WE'VE COME FOR YOUR SEARCH HISTORY
—for Myron

King Tut turns to Alan Turing & asks, "How would I test the IQs
of the Terracotta Warriors?" Turing, in time, replies: "Delicately.
" Tactics, a catalyst, a tessellation textbook: In this window seat,
13-F, I'm afraid if I sneeze I may fall outta this airplane. "Every
-thing exists," a father in the next row says to his son. "You just
gotta find it. Adventure," he persisted, "is essential. It, it's some-
where." Dark matter scavenger hunt. Is grounds for soaring, for
appetite is involved. Iditarod dogs are smarter than your iPhone.
About as spiritual as a wishing well, as odd as G-d & as strange
as Fate has been: I follow my dreams—& then plead with them.

WE'VE COME FOR YOUR MELODIOUS THUNK

"Play it wrong and make it right."

—*T.S.M.*

For in a quiet town that'd one day become home, temporarily
, to Jack Kerouac, and googled: the future birthplace of Sugar
Ray Leonard, Thelonious Monk's mother went out for a walk.
Actually, she was not his mother yet. She was merely (and the
lovely) Barbara Monk of Rocky Mount, North Carolina—But
she was, in fact, Thelonious Monk's *wife*—Thelonious Monk
Sr., that is. But he wasn't a "Sr." yet either—It was all before
little lion Thelonious was born. *Anyway*... Barbara went for a
walk, and while admiring the shape of the sun, she thought, "
Sphere would make a great middle name for a baby one day."

WE'VE COME FOR YOUR UNMISTAKEN IDENTITY

"We only kill each other."
—*Benjamin "Bugsy" Siegel*

Chingachgook, when the synagogue asked if I was of the Levite tribe, I lied. An assistant to the priests? Said no—Prior to suicide , Grandpa Ben's father was; so he was; so his son is; so I am—A pronounced *seagull* with a pronounced Adam's apple, too apprehensive to go before my students and scrabble the second prayer for the Torah reading—Weak sauce, and a birthright: lost—With the loopiness of a *kibitzer*, Grandpa Ben added a second 'l' when signing his marriage certificate. Maverick scavenger hunt—Now 36, unmarried, if I don't have a child, his name then won't either.

WE'VE COME FOR YOUR SUPPLY & DEMAND

"You are nameless. The ease of
everything is priceless."
—*André Breton*

Bestsellers. Driving the Jersey-succession of strip malls,
our roads cart like supermarket aisles. Shelves a chronic
collage of proper nouns. "However," notes the radio, "it
is still unclear if ingesting that much Pepsi actually lead
to the victim's epileptic episode." Turn signal. Seriously
, how much of life attaches to a tag? [My big toe itches.]
Don't ask—Store manager scavenger hunt. I change the
station: "*And she's buying a stairway to heaven.*" Weird.
Indebted. I mean, how much did my birth cost? It's as if
the grand total of everything that a servant of our culture
needs must be paid for. But, from *pre-sale* to *sold out*, if
I owe, then how can I own?—Watson thot Sherlock was
applauding... but all it was was him packing his tobacco.

WE'VE COME FOR YOUR MIRACULOUS MENORAH OIL

"Each body has its art."
—*Gwendolyn Brooks*

What we know about dinosaurs we know because Jesus saved
for us the information? What sound your sin? My worms ain't
ready to roar through me just yet. Can I borrow your Christmas
lights? Cadaver scavenger hunt—And what if those headstones
doubled as the tips of icebergs? Is that what happens when you
start seeing the DNA as if it's arranged by a deranged designer?
My boss just said, "We're spectacularly close to hitting ignition
on the next calamity." Mind if I pull over? I'm almost outta gas.

WE'VE COME FOR YOUR BURIED TREASURE

"I looked at my hands to see if I
was the same person."

—*Harriet Tubman*

All my life my father told me to save my shekels. Now he's all, "If you don't spend any money, you don't do anything." Another learned neuroticism no longer applicable. Fantastic. The waitress asks, "May I take your order?" and waits while her ostrich tattoo stupefies. It's script: «*head home*» I tip my fitted green Phillies hat—Lack of awareness scavenger hunt —then down it over my eyes. Under the red EXIT sign, a Dr. Jekyll-type character looks like he's pondering what happens when "Good riddance" is said to everything he's kept hidden . Interesting. Probably be a good idea for me to find out, too.

WE'VE COME FOR YOUR LATE NIGHT LIT

> "I hope the exit is joyful and I hope
> never to return."
>
> —*Frida Kahlo*

In a dream last night, the MFA mafia amputated my right arm.
In a dream last night, just before the MFA mafia amputated my
right arm, a woman with bad posture got me to straighten mine.
Rimbaud goes: "What's the toll on old Whitman's bridge?" Jay
Uxtapo quips: "'MONEY CREATES TASTE'—Jenny Holzer."
I gotta tap MAC. Whaddaya think, Wawa? Right on, let's hit it.
"Knick-knack paddywhack, give a dog a bone" scavenger hunt.
Open 24 hours. "If I kiss your ass," a critic in the corner laughs,
"yer gonna get cooties!" O what are we supposed to do with all
these receipts? That Dos Equis dude doesn't always read words
, but when he does, he prefers Poetry: "Stay quirky, my friends."

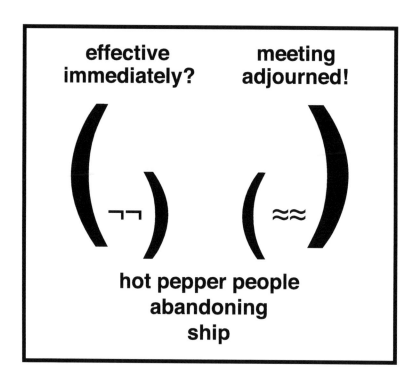

Pg. 13 rips a phrase from the PHiSH song, "The Sloth,"
and then ends on one from something Luke Kasdan-Codd once said
Pg. 15 is secretly for Brenda McLaughlin, after a terrific coincidence
Pg. 17 lifts its quote from an update that Avi Steinhardt once posted
Pg. 19 is secretly also for Jean-Michel Basquiat's *Pez Dispenser*
Pg. 25 is secretly for Steven Allen May
Pg. 27 is secretly for Kevin Varrone
Pg. 31 is secretly for Bojan "my name is my body" Louis, Fernando
Pérez, and Ryan Sibley
Pg. 41 is secretly for Stefen Wojnarowski
Pg. 46 is secretly for Molly Messana, Erin Cloud, and Kate Killian
Pg. 48 is secretly for Loud Julia
Pg. 49 is secretly for John Jacob Jingleheimer Schmidt
Pg. 56 is secretly for Tony Mancus
Pg. 57 is secretly for Larry Robin and Robin's Bookstore
Pg. 58 is secretly for Jacob Russell and owes a debt to Gil Scott-Heron
Pg. 65 is secretly for Francisco Santoni and the Grateful Dead's
"Ramble On Rose"
Pg. 74 is secretly for Jeff Newdeck
Pg. 75 lifts a lick from the PHiSH song, "Harpua"
Pg. 76 is secretly for Goose
Pg. 79 is secretly for ZOOM180, circa 2004
Pg. 98 is secretly for Jason Nagel
Pg. 99 credits Lauren Richardson with helping it find its place—
And this entire thing is secretly for Bob Dylan's "Desolation Row"

Paul Siegell's middle name is Michael, which is pretty funny. He's the author of ***wild life rifle fire*** (Otoliths, 2010), ***jambandbootleg*** (A-Head Publishing, 2009), ***Poemergency Room*** (Otoliths, 2008), & thanks to Spuyten Duyvil, this offering in 2018. Performance vids & book trailers are up on YouTube, Goodreads stars reviews, & kindly search "paul siegell wrote these shirts" for some minimalist concrete poetry merch: Razzle-dazzle scavenger hunt? *Absolutely*—Born & loved on Long Island, BA'd & BS'd at the University of Pittsburgh, & then employed as a copywriter in Orlando, Atlanta, & now Philadelphia, Paul is a senior editor at *Painted Bride Quarterly* & has contributed to *American Poetry Review*, *Bedfellows*, *Berkeley Poetry Review*, *Black Warrior Review*, *E-Verse Radio*, & other fine journals & anthologies.

ReVeLeR @ eYeLeVeL
paulsiegell.blogspot.com